The Last Man To Let You Down

The Last Man To Let You Down

You Down

by

Ernest Taylor

Finavon Print & Design

First published in Great Britain in 1996 by
Finavon Print & Design
3 Cadgers Path
Finavon, Angus DD8 3QB

Reprinted 2002

Typesetting & design by Finavon Print & Design

Covers: Andy Gourlay

Illustrations: Ron Forbes
Nature Diary story reproduced by kind permission of Colin Gibson

ISBN 0 9528813 0 6

Contents

Mother and Father

This was the Authors introduction to losing his loved ones.
Their grave stone as shown stands in Branxton Churchyard
beside Flodden Field with its memorial on the hilltop
overlooking the burial ground.

In the older part is situated a very small church, quaint both
for its interior and exterior.

The parents passing was a real family tragedy leaving five
sons and one daughter. She was the eldest and their ages
ranged from 1 to 12.

Fortunately there was one at hand to take on the role of
both Father and Mother, the mother's sister, Maggie, a lady
with a capital L. The daughter went through college to
become a teacher and every boy learned a trade. After 95
years Maggie passed away having earned every day of her
long life.

In Memory of

WILLIAM TAYLOR
WHO DIED AT MARDON 9 MAY 1924
AGED 38 YEARS.
Also ELIZABETH MITCHELL his wife
WHO DIED AT MINDRUM 11 NOV 1924
AGED 39 YEARS.

Introduction

People often say to me, "When and why did you become an undertaker." That is a long story.

In 1947 I bought over the local joiner and undertaking business. At that time the only thing going for it was the undertaking. I bought it to build up the joinery side with no intentions of undertaking whatsoever. Everything in the workshops I could buy at valuation if I wished. I asked the valuator to put the undertaking cupboard, a large pine cupboard full of all the equipment for undertaking, into the sale as I had no intentions of being an undertaker. This was duly done and I took over the work shop. I had been in the business about two weeks. There was a large wall with two big gates at the front of the workshop. Through the gates one day walked a very reverend gentleman wearing a black tie, and dark grey suit. He asked if I was the joiner and undertaker I replied, "No, I am the joiner, I don't do undertaking". He added, "That's an afa' pity as my father has just died. Your future mother in law sent me and she thought that you would help me out".

This put a slightly different light on things. I had to think very fast and think again. He asked how long I would need. I told him I would be two hours. Nowadays it would be immediately.

I was still uncertain about carrying out his wishes but

on arriving home I was told in no uncertain manner by my old aunt to go back carry out my duties. I had taken on the workshop and the undertaking was very much part of it .She duly made me the required dress for the deceased. I cycled back to the workshop not frightened at what I had to do but frightened in case I didn't do it right. There is a lot more to undertaking than meets the eye.

On arrival at the house I was blessed as the district nurse was already there. I told her I was just handing in what was required for the last rights. She said "You'll better come in, I want to see you a minute". That was the beginning of the undertaking career.

Funerals have changed greatly since these days. The funeral was done from the house and the deceased remained in the house until the day of the funeral.

I was fortunate to know of a reverend gentleman, Mr W. Adam who was a very well known undertaker in Brechin I phoned him and asked for advice with regards to the transport, papers, ground, and everything else connected with the funeral business. He said, and I will never forget his words, "Remember if you have to be an undertaker, it never was a job. Always remember it as a service to the next of kin and you will never go wrong. Consider it a job and it just won't work". These words I have carried with me until today.

He helped me with the first funeral but as so often happens the good Lord put me in at the deep end and I had three funerals within ten days.

As I have said before funerals have changed greatly since 1947. For instance, a cremation was £3 10s, whereas today it is £250. A funeral was carried out at the price of £14 to £15, but today we are approaching nearer the £1000.

This is an introduction to what I intend to put into a little book to share the lighter side of undertaking. Remember, it is not meant to make light of this profession knowing full well when a bereavement takes place it's always somebody's buddy.

I believe that everbody should dress properly according to their profession. There is nothing better for the next of kin than to see the undertaker well dressed. I was always told that irrespective of what post you take, to dress for it as you should be dressed. I think that carries through to this day.

Things have greatly changed since I started the undertaking in 1946. For instance at that time our coffins came by train to the station. I had no transport except a two wheeled joiner's barrow to bring coffins from the station. We waited till dusk when possible, and brought them to the work shop. They were wrapped in a heavy duty canvas wrapping that was returned to the suppliers after the coffin had been removed.

Most of the funerals in the village were walking funerals from the house. It was nothing unusual to have the hearse and three limousines. Today that has greatly changed because nearly everybody is mobile, with their own transport which saves a great expense for limousines.

It was much later before we began to use the church as a place for funeral services. It is much more comfortable for the mourners attending the funeral, not only that many more can be admitted to the church, but on a cold day it is warm and comfortable where the congregation can sing. Early on, it was quite common for the coffin to be carried to the local cemetery. This was carried on what they call 'spokes' by four or eight bearers when carrying for a long distance.

As you made your way to the cemetery if any of the bearers felt they needed a rest someone would just step in without having to stop to change over. Remember in these days the mourners came to the house, as I have already explained. When the house was full, the rest of the mourners remained outside bearing up to the very cold weather depending on the time of year. They would walk to the cemetery and be exposed to the elements, then return to the house where they were invited for a very welcome cup of tea and usually a 'dram' to get the circulation back to normal. Sometimes even a meal with steak pie etc.

This still carries on today, usually to a hotel and I

think it's a custom of the olden days which has been continued and is very welcome. This being the age of the motorised transport with so many people having there own cars it's now a risk to have alcohol and drive. In the olden days they either walked, cycled, came by pony and trap or whatever when they could have a dram without risking drinking and driving.

Whenever a funeral had to be arranged we had our own local grave digger. There was never any 'hassle' and we worked as a team on these occasions. I would meet the grave digger to tell him what had happened and who had passed away. Nine times out of ten the reply would be. "That's right, that's Mr so - and - so. There's two in lair one and there's nobody in lair two" and that was without looking at any book. He knew the burial ground so well he could tell you whether there was ground available or not.

Although I have reminisced about the days of the old grave digger this in no way means that we don't have good service today. From the various regions or areas the service I can assure you as far as I am concerned is first class.

The reason that I walk in front of the hearse if there are people walking behind is that it acts as a pacemaker for them and keeps the walking at a reasonable rate. If there is nobody walking I like to walk a short distance from the church or whatever to show my respects at the pace the deceased would have walked.

The new crematorium situated in central Angus will be a great asset for the rural areas. This will save on expense for transport etc. and in time in lost working hours by people who attend the funeral. This will be a great 'boon' especially travelling a distance today with a number of cars following the hearse. It is getting very dangerous with the amount of traffic on the roads. One reason is that the mourners trying to keep up with the hearse get way- laid and in panic try to force their way through traffic which could cause a very serious accident.

Not only traffic causes problems, the weather can certainly cause havoc as well if you are travelling a distance.

My earliest recollection of a funeral was seeing the hearse drawn by two lovely black horses with the hooves blackened, their harness beautifully polished and wearing long black plumes attached to the bridles on the top of their heads. Another thing that stands out in my memory was looking at the lovely polished glass case where the coffin lay, with it's ornamental carvings on the glass and the pulled down blinds slightly drawn, it's tassels just showing and no more. I remember so well thinking to myself as a wee lad, "I wonder what it's like to be in there," It looked so beautiful. It was so fascinating to see these wonderful horses and the groom sitting high with his top hat holding the reigns ready to guide these lovely animals to wherever they were going. The glass case gleaming with the flowers on top looked like a little garden.. Behind the glass case hearse came the handsome cab, a one horse drawn carriage to seat four people mostly for the next of kin. Following that was the various modes of transport, possibly pony & trap, gigs, governor cars etc.,., all horse drawn. I also remember the horse getting impatient while waiting and scraping their feet on the road giving their message that they were ready to go. When somebody passed away at that time every blind in the house was drawn and in the village many more in respect to the deceased and the family also. A common sight was to see black diamonds sewn on the sleeves of the men and the boys which were worn for a certain period of time after the funeral.

On attending the funeral it was common practice for the mourners attending to wear top hats and frock coats. That was usually the dress of the day. If not top hats and frock coats you would see bowler hats and dark suits, but everyone was dressed for the occasion. The ladies always dressed in black complete with hats and veils. The dress was important in those days. The ladies never attended the service at the cemetery but remained at the house, some helping to prepare teas. They would visit the cemetery later. Even in my early days as an undertaker, respect was number one. When the hearse went up the street the majority of people stopped and paid there last respects.

Passing through a country lane in the heart of rural areas the ploughmen stopped at the end of the field with their horses irrespective of what they were doing. They would turn toward the cortege and touch or remove their head-gear. Today things have changed, and everybody is in such a hurry that respect for the dead in many cases is forgotten. Another custom that has gone with time is that if you were invited to a funeral and received a cord for lowering the coffin into the grave, it was common practice for the bearer of the cord to take his knife and cut the tassel from the end of the cord, in remembrance of the deceased. This would be taken home and put away religiously in a drawer as a memory and honour of the occasion.

Funeral in a blizzard

One of the many bad days stands out in my memory.
I had a funeral from a village to a small hamlet in
Aberdeenshire, in all approximately 140 miles. The day
before the funeral was one big blizzard. I suppose I looked
out of the window of my house several times during the
night thinking of the long hazardous journey en-route to
the church where the service was being held. The road was
cleared by the snow ploughs leaving the snow banked high
at either side. It was six inch deep rutted snow to drive on,
all the way to the north.

The mourners came to the service by tractors and
many strange modes of transport in their working clothes
complete with wellies etc. The roads were so bad all the
way it was a hair raising experience. To make things worse
my driver who was getting on in years had just had
cataract surgery on his eyes. With the bright snow he was
being blinded and found it difficult to drive. I still maintain
the snow banked up at either side of the road kept us on
course.

At this point I'd like to add a little ditty. The driver
made a remark that the road had certainly improved and
that it was much wider with very little snow only to discover
an aircraft flying over us very low. We realized then that we
were on the runway of an airfield! This of course is

an addition to the hazardous journey. This part is funny but I can assure you the rest of the journey as I have already said was hair raising.

After all the hazards we arrived one minute early, enjoyed a very welcome cup of tea, a dram and headed for home facing heavy snow and gusting winds. The two hours normal homeward journey had taken us four and a half hours. All I could say was "It's good to be home."

Two Farmers

Two Farmers

While we were having a cup of tea after a funeral a local gentleman told me the story about the two farmers who were very jealous of each other. Living in neighbouring farms there was always competition, who was first.
The farms being in view of each other they would both watch to see who would be first with the harvest, ploughing, potatoes or whatever.

Andrew was the farmer up the hill while Jim was lower down and to his dying day Andrew was always first with everything. He duly passed away but Jim didn't go to his funeral, just for spite. Sometime later Andrew's son was in the cemetery, and noticed his father's head stone was leaning at an angle, caused by the elements. Beside the stone was a tree. He found a piece of rubber covered cable, tied it around the stone and fixed it to the tree to keep the headstone upright.

One day Jim said to his wife, "I must go down to the cemetery and make my peace with Andrew even though he was always first in everything." On return he said "I never stopped at his grave, "But why" said his wife. He replied, "Even today he embarrassed me. Looking around the cemetery I noticed he's the only one that has the phone in. First as usual."

Horse drawn Lorry at the funeral of David Lindsay Carnegie, Laird of Kinblethmont to private burial ground at Chapelton of Boysack in 1935

Too far at 90

Another story I suppose concerning transport was told to me by one of our local ministers. He was speaking to one of his parishioners who is 90 years old and still a very independent lady. In conversation he said, "What do you think of the new crematorium being built two miles down the road from you. Are you in favour of this new crematorium being built?" She replied "Well the other one is 22 miles away and I feel it is just far enough to travel at my age."

It's a small world

It is a small, a very small world. Thirty years have passed since a funeral of a high ranking officer in the police force died in Angus but was being interred in Riddrie Cemetery Glasgow. The night before the funeral I removed the deceased to his son's house where we sat there chatting, and had a very welcome cup of cocoa. The grandson of the deceased who was approximately 8 years old was asked to go and see his grandfather who was in his coffin in the next room. Personally, I don't believe a young mind should be put to such stress and therefore persuaded him that if he came with me I would give him a pen which I had been presented with. This was an early 'biro' with a clear plastic top which when turned upside down, the snow covered a 'wee' man inside the tube. He was fascinated. I walked him past the door keeping him out of view of the coffin. The funeral was carried out the next day complete with police escort, everything going to plan.

Thirty years later my wife and I were on our last night of our holiday and decided to look for a bed and breakfast in Oban. I stopped at the first sign only to discover the rooms had been taken but she said there was a lady she knew who might take us in. After a phone call we were in luck travelling past McCabes Folly. We arrived at this bungalow built on the top of the hill overlooking the bay, a most wonderful view. The lady having greeted us at the door, showed us to the lounge where the usual introductions took place. She asked me where we came from and I told her. She said her grandfather died in that village. The undertaker had dark wavy hair and wore a lum hat. On learning her grandfather's name I told her I was that undertaker.

At the time of the funeral her father was studying for the ministry. The day we arrived in Oban he had just retired and the family were going on holiday to Jerusalem. The young grandson to whom I gave the pen was now working in a government post and still had his pen from all those years ago. The sister who was only 6 years old at the time remembered so well the story of the pen. That sister was our hostess during our stay.

The Oban food I can assure you that night was good, the chat was in the past and the bed was of the best. Her parting words to me were, "I bet you got cocoa that night" and she was right. At that time her husband was an architect and herself a school teacher with one little girl. It's a small world.

Same name different address

A very sad occasion comes to my mind and what happened was an overlook by the medical authorities. I had a funeral from one of our local villages.

The party concerned was a very well respected person in the community and may I say always organised in whatever she was asked to do in life. We were at the house where the funeral service was being conducted. After the service everybody concerned was shown to their cars ready for moving off to the cemetery. Everything was in order for the journey only to discover the driver could not move the hearse because an ambulance had just arrived and was blocking our exit. At this point the ambulance driver stepped out and said that he had come to pick up so - and - so. I unfortunately had to reply that the person concerned was in the hearse ready for the last journey. He then told me that he had come to take her to the hospital. To this day I feel sorry for that ambulance driver. He was three days too late and heart breaking for all concerned. As it turned out the name was the same but the address was wrong.

Phantom Aircraft

The phantom aircraft

One of the most memorable occasions was the funeral
of a great friend of mine who like myself served in the
Royal Air Force during the war. He was a full time
navigator on Lancaster Bombers, which was a very hard
slog. He and I had many long discussions concerning the
junior core of the services that being the Royal Air Force.
He was a flight lieutenant with various awards for
gallantry, which I might add was never part of his discussions.
He was a hero without comment, completed 30 bombing
raids over Germany and as he said survived with great
difficulty. As the saying goes he had been through the mill
and back many times.

The day of his funeral I was sitting in prayer in the
church. During the serviceI wondered if I had done my
duties as I should have done. No, I thought there should
have been recognition apart from what was
happening in the church. By this I meant what a nice gesture
it would have been,to have some recignition shown as a last
respect to a great member of our air crew who did so much
for so little during the war.
I thought I should have contacted possibly our local air
base and asked the commanding officer for a small
recognition for his great services to his King and Country.
This I can assure you was in my prayers. It was too late.

The service in the church was completed and we arrived at the cemetery where the interment was to take place. I had already expressed my disappointment to the minister concerned about the fact that I could have done more about a small flypast. Even a small private aircraft just to give a 'wee waggle' on his wings in respect and acknowledgement for his services rendered.

The interment was carried out with this still in my mind that what I had omitted I could have done in recognition of his flying days in the Royal Air Force. With this very much in my thoughts I imagined I heard the engines of an aircraft resembling a Lancaster Bomber. I could not believe my eyes and my ears as we all stood to attention after the committal was completed, I looked up and like the mourners was completely dumbfounded. A Hercules aircraft of the Royal Air Force was approaching us at approximately 200 feet and flew over the grave with it's lovely silent engines. The pilot who was easily seen dipped his wing in respect and recognition.

As we were chatting about this amazing coincidence the next of kin thanked me for organising the flypast. I said in respect, "I have never organised any flypast, but I can assure you I had thought a lot about what I should have done and didn't do."
Needless to say my heart and eyes were filled with loving tears both for the honour bestowed on my friend but also

for the fact my prayers were answered.

To tell the next of kin this was an impossibility. They would not believe me but insisted that I had arranged it. Needless to say I was quite surprised and shocked with what had happened and had to find out why this wonderful aircraft at this important part of the service was there to pay its last respects.

As I made inquiries from the local RAF station I was advised it had come from down south. There was denial that it was ever arranged by any member of the squadron he served with in Lancasters.

On contacting the air base from where the plane supposedly came it was explained that there were lots of Hercules aircraft on training flights all over Britain. I said it was very unusual that an aircraft of that calibre to come straight up the valley which to me was right off the usual flight path. In answer he said, "I can assure you their were none of our aircraft in that area at that time nor would they be on that course."

We are left today with the phantom aircraft paying its last respects to a guy who was real in ever sense of the word.

The story will never be solved in fact I think, as it stands, it is the best way to leave it.

I still put my hands to God in thanks for recognising what I was asking for and on behalf of everybody concerned I pray the phantom Hercules keeps dipping its wings, just a little, in respect to who ever it may concern.

Smoke Alarm

Smoke alarm

One fine day I had a funeral to a local cemetery. On this occasion the hearse was brand new, the value being approximately £24,000. It was very nice to be in the company of such a vehicle and that my driver was wearing his brand new suit of striped trousers and black jacket.

When we arrived at the cemetery the hearse went up to the graveside where the flowers were to be removed.

As I walked past the vehicle I caught a glimpse of a pall of smoke coming from the front seat. My immediate thoughts were that the new machine was on fire. I went around to the undertaker's side. My driver was removing a large wreath from the front with smoke getting worse.

I said, "Where's the smoke coming from.." He replied, "I don't know." He started to jump up and down saying," I'm on fire! I'm on fire! "

What happened while he was leaning over the front seat for the flowers was that a new box of matches in his trouser pocket was ignited with the pressure against the seat.

I asked if his trousers were burnt, He replied, "No, but there is something else scorched."

To see the damage it was going to be rather embarrassing especially with the folk standing around. He had flashed enough without going public.

Approximately one week had passed when we were at a hotel some miles away having a meal. I went up to the bar for drinks when a voice said, "Trust the rural undertaker to be first to try it out." This gentleman being the city undertaker I couldn't quite understand what he meant. On returning to the bar I said, "I'm not quite with you." He then replied, "I believe you are now doing grave side cremations." How news travels! I was sure my friend and I were the only ones who were involved but you never know.

Dead man answers the door

My wife and I were invited to have dinner with another couple in a hotel near Perth approximately three quarters of an hour travelling time from our place of business. The meal was being served when the waiter came to say a Mr Taylor was wanted on the telephone.

After a short discussion my services were required as someone had been in an accident which turned out to be fatal. Leaving my sirloin steak which was staring at me with that tender look I was on my way leaving the rest of the company at the hotel.

On arriving at the scene the party concerned was just leaving in the ambulance. I then began to make the usual inquiries, speaking to the police about which hospital he had gone to etc. They told me who he was and that one of the witnesses was a great friend of his and worked beside him every day of the working week. Having good witnesses to identify made things easy. The driver of the car was shocked but he could not have avoided the accident as the now deceased had walked in front of the vehicle.

After a short comforting discussion with him the worst still had to come.

The police sergeant asked if I would notify the next of kin.

I replied, "I think that is a job for the police," I did agree to accompany him to the house.

As he rang the door bell we waited. At last a gentleman came to the door and said, "I've been waiting for someone to call and tell me that I was killed in an accident. Just hang on and I'll let the Mrs know she can make the arrangements for my funeral."
Looking at me he added, "A disappointing undertaking for you." The policeman, to say he was shocked was putting it mildly and was I flabbergasted!
Oh yes! I knew that steak had a smirk when I left it.
The sergeant and I walked back keeping our thoughts to ourselves then he said, "You know undertaker at least there is one good thing, that chap will be glad he is still alive." The reason he was waiting for someone to arrive at the house was that one of the locals had heard of the accident and went to console his wife.

Needless to say the deceased lived for many happy years after the incident and ever time I met him he would say, " I'm no quite ready yet."
I spoke with the man who did the identifying and asked him, "What made him so sure of the identification?" He said, "He had a bald 'heed' and a half bottle of rum in his pocket.." Aye, that is the way to recognise your friends.
I got the wrong man and my opposition got the funeral.
What a mistake!

The hirer forgot

One of these days when things went slightly wrong.
The funeral was being carried out quite local the service
being held in the house before travelling thereafter to the
Crematorium. It was in the days when few people had their
own transport and the next of kin supplied a limited
number of limousines.
In this case it was the hearse and three limousines.
The service had begun in the house with most of the
mourners under cover and as usual I went to stand at the
door to control anything that was required from the
outside.

On checking my watch I realised the hearse and three
cars hadn't arrived. Being quite near to the office I phoned
the party concerned regarding the vehicles. A panic stricken
reply came over the phone I forgot to book the transport. I
will be there in a 'jiffy'.
Alas! there were nine miles between me and this 'jiffy'.
By the time the minister had finished they arrived. The car
drivers couldn't leave their seats as they still had their
working boots and trousers on, covered over with their
raincoats. One of the mourners said to me, "What happened
that they were late?"

I had to tell a white lie by saying the hearse which

was a Rolls Royce with large chrome wheel discs had a puncture and that was the reason.

We travelled the 23 miles to the crematorium and arrived just in time. I thought how easy it was to get out of the difficulty.

On returning the mourner who had previously asked about the vehicles being late said, "You shouldn't tell a lie. I am in the hiring limousine business and therefore took the privilege to check your hearse, I can assure you there hasn't been any of your wheels removed. All the wheel discs are showing the same amount of grime and there are no finger-prints on any of them which there would have been if any of the wheels had been removed. It is just a point worth remembering."

I was certainly caught out with my little white lie - there's always one.

Irish Funeral Director

There are so many light-hearted things that are said in this profession not more so than the story of the Irish funeral director. He was attending to the village character who had just died. After having dressed him for his last journey he required three chairs to lay the body on. The bedroom upstairs was adjacent to an open balcony leading to the basement where all the mourners were having a rehearsal for the wake. The undertaker shouted downstairs, could you put up three chairs (cheers) for Willie. They replied, hip hooray, hip, hip hooray.

A Lie on the rollers

A lie on the rollers

Another story that's told is about the funeral that was carried out, approximately ninety miles to travel. The weather was really foul, with very strong gale force winds and driving rain. After the service was completed it was as they say, "Home James and don't spare the horses." In other words, let's get back over the ninety miles as quick as possible. The weather had never let up, in fact it was deteriorating, when into the headlights of the hearse came the figure of a man. You can imagine the scene, pitch dark lashing rain and gale force winds. The figure was that of a sailor complete with his kit bag. They stopped and asked him if he would like a lift, and he accepted. The undertaker told him there were only three seats and they were all occupied, the driver, the minister and himself, but if he didn't mind travelling on the rollers in the back he was welcome. Without hesitation the door was opened and he was in. After a journey of fifty miles through violent storms they were reaching habitation, a small town. The sailor seeing the lights thought he would have a cigarette and lit up. The headroom in the back being very limited he had to lie on his back or turn on his side. As they got into the centre of the town he couldn't see as the glass was steamed up, so he decided to clean the glass with his hand. Just as he was doing this two or three senior citizens were standing as they came up to the halt sign. When looking at the hearse there in front was the full staff to carry out any funeral. With the sailor in the back who they thought was waving to draw attention with the glow of a cigarette. One old chap said, "You know it's one thing being efficient but that's ridiculous, the poor chap still waving and smoking a cigarette." The other man said, "And a cut price job, no coffin, what are things coming to." It goes on to say that when they arrived at their destination the undertaker opened the back door and had to practically lift him out. As they proceeded to straighten his legs he said, "Well, that's the coldest journey I've ever had." The undertaker replied , "You're the first person to come out of there and complain. " A chilly affair but at least it was dry, ship ahoy.

The lost grave

This is a story about a lady who approached her husband about a holiday in Canada. He said, "Had the finances been better we could have both gone but that can't be, so just you pack your case and get your ticket for a six week stay with your relative." He duly took her to the airport and bade her farewell knowing she wouldn't be able to return for six weeks, that being the condition of her ticket. She arrived in Canada to enjoy a much appreciated change. She had been there for three weeks when she got word her husband had died . Knowing the terms of her flight she had to run the full six weeks before she could return. When she came back the funeral had passed and in the very large cemetery didn't know where he had been buried. She asked the cemetery attendant at the lodge where her husband was interred. "What was his name?" he asked and she answered that he was known mostly as Jock. He replied, "That doesn't help me much at all, anything else?" "Oh yes," she said "his second name was Broon, "He added," Jock Broon, that doesn't ring a bell either. Is there anything at all that you can think about that would bring this to my mind?" "Yes" she said,"He always said to me if ever I was unfaithful to him he would turn in his grave." "Ah," said the attendant," I know exactly who you are speaking about. Now I know where the grave is,It's away down the far corner.He's aye turnin. We ca' him birler broon."

Medication Required

Medication required

The driver of a hearse was going to a funeral and going through his pockets he discovered his cigarettes were finished. Travelling up the steep hill he noticed a small shop at the top, stopped the vehicle, went into the shop and on his way out he met a policeman who asked him if that was his hearse. He said, "Yes, why?" He replied, "It's now on it's way down the hill in reverse." When it got to the bottom of the hill it went across a very busy road and the back of the vehicle hit the front of a chemist shop. The coffin burst through the door of the hearse through the shop window and slid along the chemist's counter hitting the back wall. On the point of impact the lid of the coffin burst open, and the body sat up and said "Anything to stop this coffin". (coughin)

Hand Drawn Hearse Circa Early 1900's.
Made by Dottridge Brothers of London, used by St Georges Church, and Parish
Burial Ground in Saham Toney Village, Norfolk. Believed to have been used
until mid 1950's.

Youre money or else

It is said of one of the older style undertakers who had difficulty with a funeral account which was six months overdue. He phoned the gentleman concerned saying he would like to discuss the matter in the cemetery at the grave where the burial had taken place. This was agreed. When the gentleman arrived there was the undertaker standing on the grave with a digging spade. After all the excuses about paying the account he asked, "Why have you brought the spade?" "Well you see," said the undertaker. "This being your last chance, it's a case of a method we use, and that is down with the dibs or up she rises."

Entering Parkgrove Crematorium Friockheim. Angus on the occassion of the first funeral, 16th April 1993. Funeral Directors, J. Farquhar, E. Taylor.

Happy birthday

Another light hearted story is about the couple who attended the funeral in the beautifully laid out country churchyard. After the service was complete they decided, it being a lovely day, to have a walk around admiring the lovely rose beds, shrubs etc. They came to a nice shaded corner with a patch of green grass. She said to her husband, "What about buying this plot for us when we pass on." He replied, "Not for me, I'm being cremated." She said, "Well, in that case What about buying it for me? My birthday is in three weeks. That would suit me." He went to the appropriate office and purchased the ground. On the day of her birthday he presented her with the ground certificate and wished her a happy birthday. Next year when her birthday came around she thought she wouldn't ask for anything too expensive just a small gift. When she told him the reply was very fast indeed, "No my lass There will be no present this year you see You never used the one I gave you last year."

Sauchiehall Street

Christmas in Sauchiehall Street

Many years ago a prominent figure of the village passed away the remains being cremated. With the ashes obtained by myself, I awaited further instructions as to where they were to be scattered or buried. It was almost Christmas when I got a phone call saying the venue for the ashes was Glasgow. He explained that his late wife belonged the area and had always done her shopping in Sauchiehall Street, especially at a very prominent shop called Pettigrew and Steven. She always said she would like her remains scattered in the street in front of that shop. My heart missed a beat on receiving the request but the service says you must always try to please. Before any time or date was fixed I thought some enquiries would be in order especially from Glasgow. I started off by phoning the police to see if it would be in order for this to be carried out. The policeman -on -duty's reply, "As long as you don't scatter them in my police office that is all right by me." The next worry was that to carry anything that resembled a small casket would be easily spotted by the onlookers. I phoned a friend of mine who is in the same business who had a container with sprinkler attached and would lend it to me. Being near Christmas he would wrap it in Christmas paper. When I arrived all I had to do was puncture the base paper and I would be ready for action. At last the date was fixed and it was unfortunate for me to have to carry this out on the day of Christmas Eve. The weather was very bad and I decided to go by rail. The deceased's husband accompanied me. There I sat in the carriage covering the sprinkler which was made of bronze and weighed what seemed a hundred weight. The nearer I got to Glasgow the worse I felt, I begun to see not my destination but Barlinnie Prison and me locked up container and all. I thought "What about the litter act? I had overlooked it and I had no proof of approval from the police." We arrived at the station to discover the weather was showing signs for the better which meant there would be more people on the streets doing their Christmas shopping. As we walked up the platform we passed the lovely big steam engine puffing and blowing steam and looking very relaxed. We came to the end of the platform. There was the porter taking the tickets. You know I felt like giving him the Christmas wrapped container and keeping the ticket. As we left the station I asked if we would call a cab. He said, "No we will walk, it isn't all that far." Not very if you are empty handed and your legs are not shaking. After a walk that seemed like eternity we arrived at the destination where I was to do the needful, boy oh boy! The day before Christmas the street was bedecked in it's festive attire complete with glaring lights.

The walkway was packed with shoppers but I thought looking at my parcel that they were just like me all carrying parcels. The street traffic was very active and to walk there would have been fatal. I now had to do what I was there for and duly punctured the paper covering the bottom of the sprinkler and walked up the street keeping to the outside of the path I thought things were going very well until two young girls behind me laden with parcels were speaking rather loudly trying to draw my attention. Eventually after my mission was complete they caught up with me explaining that my parcel had been losing it's contents for quite a distance. I carried out my duty and would prefer to forget the ordeal. Alas every year on Christmas Eve it's always with me. On the return journey my companion spent his time at the bar. He got drunk and I got ulcers.

On arriving home I discovered my services were required by a shepherd who had passed away in his little cottage. It was rather a lonely spot where there had been quite a bit of snow. On leaving the cottage I looked at the foot prints of my assistant and myself. I thought it was a long way from Sauchiehall Street and a lot less feet to avoid, I should have dressed like Santa.

The twelve cords

Some time ago when I was a very young undertaker and still had a lot to learn, but equally as much to discover that the services one is required to carry out for the future is well and truly in the unknown.

I had arranged for a funeral. The night before a telephone call was received from a gentleman from Edinburgh who said he was the family solicitor.

He asked me if another four cords could be added to the coffin this making twelve in all. It is bad enough getting eight people around the grave to lower the coffin so a lot of doubt was put in my mind about having twelve. Undertakers have to be on their guard when carrying out services as there can be somebody trying to be funny or a con as they call it today and putting the people doing this service for the public into panic or disrepute.

To see if the solicitor was genuine, he having phoned on the Sunday, for me to check back was very difficult. Understandably their office wasn't available for comment. The next best thing was the police who very kindly checked and confirmed that the party and his company of solicitors were in order. With such a strange request the seeds of doubt were still in my mind.

To make things worse I didn't have four cords or tassels to

match the other eight so I phoned a firm of funeral directors to see if they could help. They, being en- route to where we were going and being very helpful, said if we called in they would help.

When we arrived the father and boss of this family business was waiting. His words to me were, "Now then laddie just you go into the office and have a cup of coffee and we will do the rest." My driver and I enjoyed our break while the extra cords were being fitted.

I looked at the twelve tassels and the boss asked what I thought, I said,"I'm not too proud of what I see but it having been a request I don't think looks will count." He just gave me a rather strange look and we were ready to go. Speaking to me through the window from the hearse he said, " You know, my grandfather, my father, myself and also my son now have been in this business covering over approximately 150 years and I have never heard of such a thing nor have I ever seen it before. Being in the hearse ready to go on our way his words certainly did not help regarding my doubts as to whether I was doing the right thing but it was now too late.

On arrival at the cemetery I found the last resting place all ready for the service but could not see any mourners. After a walk into the old Kirkyard I found amongst others the gentleman who had phoned me and that was one big sigh of relief.

There was still one person to find and that was the minister who would be carrying out the service. I couldn't see the minister anywhere and I thought that this will possibly be the first time I've had to carry out a service without one.

At that time in case of such an occasion I always carried, stuck in the inside of my top hat, the wording needed to complete such a task. I then proceeded to carry on with my duties asking the mourners to gather round the grave, which they did. There were twelve people in total who walked over to the graveside.

I presented each with a cord with which they duly lowered the coffin and walked away while I was left standing with my top hat in hand ready to read the service that was never required.

I thought to myself, "Well now that is something different" I walked over to my solicitor friend and said," I didn't want to sound inquisitive but could you enlighten me on the way the last rights were carried out." He replied,"It's just our belief. We recognise the twelve disciples "Hence the fact there was no minister to carry out the service.

There we are, another day, another discovery.

Funeral of Alan G. Nicol, founder member of Royal British Legion, Friockheim.

The Digger that didn't

You know I don't think there is anything more
worrying to an undertaker than the dread of arriving at a
cemetery where the hole hasn't been dug, when the
minister forgets about the funeral service, that he is going to
a crematorium where he has to be at a certain arranged time
and is delayed, the organist for a church service forgets to
be there or you arrive at the cemetery to discover the grave
is too small for the coffin. These are some of the things that
a funeral director worries about while the people attending
usually give him sympathy rather than blame him for any
mistake.

Funeral directors in general are really organised to
the last straw but other people make mistakes. I waited
many years for something to go wrong outwith my control
and it did. The first was in the days when you could inter
cremated remains at any time. In this case it was a Sunday-
a beautiful spring day, lovely and peaceful, I remember
en-route looking at the bunches of growing daffodils and
thinking yes, another year another beginning. I looked over
to the cemetery noting a large crowd was waiting. Being
cremated remains we did not use a hearse but a limousine.
My driver as usual in attendance did the necessary opening
of doors etc. allowing me to step out carrying the

remains on a blue and gold pall. There was quite a long walk to the interment area. I was trying to be very reverend walking at the right pace and I looked up to find the young man standing in front of me. His exact words were,"Undertaker, there's nae hole." Without hesitation, still keeping that pace I turned around and headed back to the car. The driver said, "Where now." My throat was very dry and I said, "The nearest telephone." I phoned the grave digger concerned who was busy having his Sunday lunch when he heard my voice on the phone. There was nothing to be heard from his end except a choking sound. When he got his breath back I'm sure a great proportion of his lunch had been stuck to various items of furniture. All he could reply was "Hells bells, me to blame, I'll be right there." He had to travel approximately eight miles ,which he did in a very fast time. Meanwhile I had gone back and asked the mourners to take a walk for an hour which they obligingly did. Give the gravedigger his due he apologised and relieved me of any guilt.

The lost chord

Another embarrassing moment was if you remember
the early part of my story concerned my aunt who was
father and mother to her sisters six children, my father and
mother both dying at the age of thirty nine years. She was
the person who said,"You've bought the business, now get
on with it." Had that not been so I would not have been
writing this book today. We have all heard of the lady with
the lamp. She had a lamp and lit it with parental love.
She always, before I went out to do a funeral prior to my
marriage, would make sure I remembered everything, the
organist, the minister, you name it. She had it on her list. At
the time of her death aged ninety four years, the only time
the organist was not playing was the day of her service.
The minister said he would arrange for the organist but
admitted he forgot. You know God moves in mysterious
ways. The congregation at the church sang their hearts out
without the music and the one who never let me forget
wasn't forgotten. Now all those years have passed and its
the only time it has happened.

Absent-minded Minister

We now come to the minister who forgot about the service being held in his own church. Everything was in order as planned. My staff were at the church thirty minutes before the service was due to start and the organist had been playing for some time. As usual I went to the vestry to bring the minister in to take the service but alas all I found was an empty chair. Allowing for some delay I waited ten minutes having notified the congregation what was happening. In case there would be no minister I phoned one of my undertaking friends who rushed a retired minister to the church and who was prepared to help me out. Waiting for him to arrive seemed to take ages. The organist kept strumming away while I kept in touch with the mourners. I contacted a senior elder to ask him if it would be in order to take the service being an elder myself. He told me that would not be allowed. I discovered later that I could have carried out a service with a memorial talk and a couple of hymns.

Almost thirty minutes had passed when both the ministers arrived together. The one who forgot said to me to let the retired one do the service. Being so annoyed at his forgetfulness I said, "Your duty awaits you in the pulpit. Get going and remember the apology for forgetting to be here as arranged." Being quite near to the cemetery I had someone keep in touch with the attendants as to how things were developing at my end. It was told to me by someone who was waiting at the cemetery that the minister, knowing he was late, went to the gravediggers and his words were, "I don't think I can face the undertaker after what has happened." The gravedigger replied, "Well minister, the undertaker has kept us in the picture and if I were you I'd get along to the church, He'll no be putting the deceased down. It's you who'll go into the hole." Apologies work for some things but I think for a minister who was thirty minutes late because he forgot to look at his diary was a very **GRAVE** situation.

Friendship restored

Speaking of my parents, they were laid to rest in a lovely little church yard at Branxton in Northunberland beside Flodden field where the battle was fought. The church is very small but to me it is really different. We visit the grave quite regular, and always have a glance through the visitors' book. That book was the means of a broken friendship being repaired. I had a great friend who knew my situation regarding to where my parents were buried etc. After many years as great pals we unfortunately drifted apart for a time. Very little was said between us, however, unknown to me he and his wife had been travelling from the south and noticed the sign to Branxton. Remembering my story they called in and went into the church signing the visitors book. My wife and I were there one week later and I was so proud to think that they had paid their respects and signed the visitors book in the church. I just had to call him to say how nice it was they had been at the cemetery. We were after that again the best of friends, not only with him but his whole family. Alas he died some years ago. I was asked to carry out his funeral which I did and I can assure you with great difficulty.
Losing his friendship saddened me and for why or what? Now there are two memorials in that little church yard one

at the time with a happy ending the other well who knows
we still have to get there.

No money, no help

My phone rang one day and at the other end was a lady who was in charge of a Care Centre for the Elderly, to say a resident had died. She explained to me that there were no known funds available but that the lady concerned had ground which had been purchased by her parents many years before and she named the cemetery where she was to be buried. Then she added, "Now that you know the circumstances would you be prepared to do her funeral free of charge?" At this time there was a funeral grant which was far from being adequate to pay for the expenses. I thought, "Surely as we go through life maybe just that bit luckier than some folk, why not?" I said, " Yes." She thanked me and we got down to the final arrangements for the funeral day. The night before the day of the funeral I received a phone call from a solicitor who in the past had handled the affairs of the deceased's family. He stated there were no funds available and that if I or any other party concerned with the funeral arrangements sent him an account he wouldn't accept any debts or any expenses incurred whatsoever and that his firm would not be liable. I never told him what arrangements the lady of the Care Centre and I had come to.

The funeral duly took place. After the service I was

walking away from the grave when a lady approached me and asked if she could have a word in private. We walked a little and at this point she handed me a brown envelope saying this was to be given to you and you only.

The message on the note emphasised this. I opened the envelope in which there was a bank book containing quite a sum of money to pay for her last rights.

She left instructions for me to pay all expenses for her funeral. As we walked through the cemetery I explained to the bearer that the deceased in her note meant well but by law as an undertaker I could do nothing about it except hand the bank book over to the Residential Home for the Elderly. By this I mean there is a procedure that has to be carried out which is bound over by the laws of the country and a good thing in many ways.

One week after the funeral my phone rang to find at the other end a voice that sounded familiar. After a couple of questions, low and behold if it wasn't my friend the law man who had already told me in no uncertain manner that there was no money and as far as he was concerned no services would be provided by him or his company for the deceased. He now went on to say that he had received funds for the old lady and for me to forward to him my account with all expenditure and that money was now no object. I told him I knew all about it as a friend of the deceased had presented me with the Bank Book. He was very much surprised. I said to him, "I have discovered since talking to you that you base your life on three things and they mean pounds, shillings and pence.

No money, no business, - plenty money, plenty business. You know we all have a cross to bear but it's nice sometimes if we can give somebody a hand to carry theirs.

We come into this world with nothing and we go out with nothing." He then proceeded to say, "You know undertaker there is a very old saying, All's well that end's well." He still had the last word.

The Mother-in-law

The mother-in-law

There is the tale of a funeral that was passing through this little village on it's way to the church yard when a bystander noticed something rather strange or at least different from other funeral processions. There was the hearse and behind it was walking a sombre looking gent being pulled along by a rather large rottweiler dog. Another strange thing was the fact that everybody attending, instead of walking abreast, were in a straight line one behind the other. The bystander thought I must find out what goes on here. He joined the chap with the dog explaining to him how he thought it was a rather unusual procession but none more so than everybody in a straight line. Then he asked who was being buried. The man replied, " My mother - in - law." He then asked if it was sudden. The gent with the dog replied, "It was very sudden, in fact my dog got her with one bite." The gent then said, "Your mother - in - law, how very sad! Is there any chance of borrowing your dog? "Aye he said, "That would be quite in order but you will have to get to the back of the queue."

Colour to order

I think this item should be her favourite colour.
This is the story of a lady who entrusted me with the
arrangements of her funeral and for many years before she
died she would keep reminding me of her wishes. One of
them was that the coffin had to be green, her favourite
colour, and she used to say that if I didn't carry out that
wish she would come back and haunt me. I told her that
this would either put my business in ruins or enhance it.
She would reply "Whatever it does you will carry out my
last wish." I promised faithfully to do that.

This lady was no fool, a very hard worker, would
walk miles to work on the local farms and I'm led to believe
could do any thing that any of the men employed there
could do. She was a great character in her self and many a
sincere chat we had. She passed away and of course for me
the difficult part had just begun. After attending to the
needs of the body I phoned my coffin supplier telling him
that the coffin had to be a dark shade of green. He said,
"Have you been ill." I said, "No" and I asked him why he
thought I'd been ill. "It's just," he said, "You seem to have
got mixed up with your colours." At this point I heard him
say to his son who was within hearing distance from the
phone. "You know it does happen I think he's gone

bammy." I made no reply what I had overheard and still insisted on what I wanted. He said, "I think the best thing to do is for me to pop down to see you." He duly arrived complete with samples painted in three shades of green. After making a choice he said, "You know I'm so glad I've seen you and you are all right. This sort of thing has never happened before and I've never heard of such a thing, I just hope it does not start a precedent and the other undertakers will request coffins in different colours. This would cause quite an upheaval."

However the day of the funeral I was walking down the street to the cemetery. To say it was different would be an understatement. On the side streets as we passed there was a lot of people standing waiting for the cortege to pass having heard of the lady's colour scheme. The night before the funeral this was so much unheard of to have a coloured coffin that the supplier came down and took a picture of the coffin. He duly sent me a copy. As time went by my guilt felt stronger in having the photo in my possession and I decided to destroy it. She did say if I didn't do everything right she would be back to haunt me. Maybe having the picture was one of the wrongs. This is another instance where we just don't know what is beyond.

A moving signal

Another tale was told of a lady who had great difficulty with her husband as Burns would have said "ane oh them that had teen tae drink". He just loved the stuff with the result his pocket was always empty. His wife remarked how she had to hide any money including her handbag to keep his clammy hands off her cash. Alas he passed on and two years later her father died and was to be buried next grave to her husband. The cemetery where this was to take place was infested with mole hills caused by the moles burrowing and pushing up the soil.
On the day of the funeral the family were all gathered around the grave to lower her father's coffin. She, having one of the cords, before she stepped over to take her cord, took her handbag off her arm and laid it on her husbands grave until the coffin had been lowered and the service was past.

The service took approximately twenty minutes. When finished she turned to pick up her handbag. She looked at the undertaker quite shocked that her bag was moving and by this time was on top of the small mound of earth.
As she picked up her bag she remarked, "My God! He's still at it. I wonder where he would have spent the cash."

Tasty floral tribute

I suppose the title of this one could be 'kidding.' A funeral service that was being held in this lovely country church with the interment later in the churchyard. As the pall bearers carrying the coffin were walking down to the grave they could hear a clanking sound, clank, clank, which was coming from what appeared to be a short distance behind. At this point the undertaker went back to bring the flowers up to the burial area. As he arrived at the gate where the flowers were laid, to his horror he discovered the clanking noise was nothing else than a billy goat that had broken itss tether but still had the chain hanging from his neck. By this time the goat had eaten quite a number of the flowers and was enjoying his meal immensely .

The undertaker just wasn't sure how to tackle the situation, the goat being quite a fearsome chap with rather large horns. Before he could grab the chain attached to the goat it took off still with a wreath in his mouth. He thought to himself that to be brave could be foolish and he allowed the goat to go on his way. Rescuing the rest of the flowers he took them down to the burial area. He thought, " I could do nothing else now but say how sorry I am to the next of kin," went up to the widow and made his apologies.
She replied, "We can't say it was an act of God but just an

unusual incident . To think my husband wasn't even a free mason ."

A typical Scottish village funeral procession where the Funeral Director walks beside the hearse.

Something fishy

Another fishy story. I'm sure you've heard the saying "Hook, line and sinker" but in this case there was no line nor sinker. This gentleman was a very keen angler who was famous for making many different kinds of flies for the hooks and supplied them to angling clubs far and wide. He was a widower and had three sons, nice hard working lads. The day of the funeral after his interment everybody was invited to have a cup of tea and wee dram at the local hotel, after which the last will and testament would be read. The family now relaxed, the solicitor said the usual as to how sad he was but his duties had to be carried out meaning the reading of the will. He said to the three boys, "You are the rightful heirs to the estate which reads as follows. To my eldest son I have left 8,000, to my middle son I leave 6,000, to my youngest son I leave 3,000. After a pause the eldest son completely surprised with this announcement turned and said to the solicitor, "Well I don't know, I never knew my father had all that money." The solicitor replied, "Oh I should have told you its nor money but fishing hooks you've been left."

Easy way down

Escape from the grave. The funeral was taking place in the local church yard and it was one of those days when the cosy fire would have been the warmest place to be. The village people ever faithful in time of need gave their support in attending the burial for one of their own kith and kin. The funeral undertaker warned all attending to be very wary of the underfoot conditions especially those at the grave side as the timber planks where they would be standing to lower the coffin were very slippery.

After the coffin was lowered he asked the pallbearers to leave the graveside and helped some of them from the slippery planks but alas, there is always one who decides to do it the other way. This gentleman did just that and decided to jump across the gaping hole. As he did so his feet slipped and at that point he fell bottom first into the grave on top of the coffin.

Unseen hilarity broke out amongst limousine drivers etc., Falling as he did across the grave the situation was funny but serious. There in the shape of a human with legs in the air he was firmly set down the hole.

The family now were helping the undertaker and staff to release him, to get him up to ground level. With a lot of pulling they eventually released him. I suppose to you it's very funny said the gentleman.

The grave digger added, "It's just so unusual for somebody to come out of a grave making rude remarks , We usually have to help them down in silence.

The Reverend Wellington

A rather large congregation was seated in the Church. The organist was playing soft music pror to the service, the Undertaker and his assistant were at the Church door awaiting the arrival of the Minister, The Rev. D. Black. He was to arrive in his own mode of transport, a rather old banger or should I say a Vintage Type Car. Zero hour had arrrived but the Reverend hadn't. The Funeral Director sent one of his limousines to the Manse only to find on arrival the gentleman concerned was digging his garden wearing his old trousers and wellies. The driver gave his horn a 'toot' and signalled him to come and speak. The Minister waved his hand and smiled then enquired what he wanted. The driver said,"You are overdue for the Service." He answered, "No, it's tomorrow." The driver continued, "There are approx. 150 people in the Church who all say it's today and are patiently waiting." "Oh well," he replied. He went into the house shaking his head, picked up his Bible and got into the Limousine. He carried out the Service in his gardening attire, wellies and all. trousers tucked in of course. After all he was only a day out. What a Wellie!

Quotes

Remember man as you pass by,
For you are now as once was I
For I am now, as you will be
Prepare thy self to follow me.

Do not stand at my grave and weep,
I am not there I do not sleep
I'm a thousand winds that blow
I'm the diamond glint on snow
I'm the sunlight on ripened grain
I'm the gentle Autumn rain
When you awaken in the morning hush
I'm the swift uplifting rush
Of quiet birds in circle flight
I'm the soft stars that shine at night
Do not stand at my grave and cry
I'm not there I did not die.

Line found in a trench during the First World War
And here we lie in earth's cauld kist
The lave live on and were never missed.

Lych-Gates

Lych-Gates like porches may be fashioned in timber or stone or a mixture of both, and are occasionally attached to a church house which at one time contained a chapel.

The use of Lych-Gates continued until the close of the eighteenth century; recently they have reappeared as a useful form of memorial.

Their origin arose as a convenient place at the entrance to the burial yard, where the bearers might deposit the coffin and rest before proceeding into the church, and where the officiating priest and clerk met the procession and from the Lych-Gate commenced the burial service. In mediaeval times few church yards were without a Lych-Gate; some had more than one as is indicated in the Wardens' accounts for Malpas, Cheshire. Timber Lych-Gates often needed renewal; in the Bunbury accounts for the seventeenth century in the same county a carpenter is paid for felling the Lych-Gate, together with timber and wages for making a new one.

Lych-Gates may be planned in two ways: one with the gables porch running with the path, the other where the Lych-Gate straddles across it. The space beneath the roof might be occupied by a single gate or by a pair; another method was to divide the space into a main gate and a side wicket. It was also arranged as a stile, with a centre post working upon a swivel to which the gate was fastened on either side, returning to the clapper after it had been pushed open. The essential thing was to have adequate protection from the weather, and when the ridge ran transversely to the path the gables were often hipped to cover all four sides.

Except when combined with a house, the ends were often exposed, that is until the eighteenth century. There remains examples of the gates being com- bined with a house, but not often a half-timbered one as Hertfield, Sussex, 1520, Chalfont St. Giles, Buckingham, and Penshurst, Kent. At Bray, Berkshire, the house contains an ancient chapel, the date on the gate being 1448.

The construction of the ends of the Lych-Gate and its divi- sion of often the characteristic feature of the gate, the curved braces supporting the roof are balanced by the splayed struts at the base, fixed into strong longitudinal cill- beams as was once at Beckenham, Kent.

Standing the test

Standing the test

Recently we were showing at a funeral and crematorium exhibition. It so happened that a firm was showing cardboard coffins, which I suppose one day will come on the market. This was a complete coffin that would be fully seen if it were used at a funeral. I would rather see them being used as a lining in an ornamental shell. The shell would return to the undertaker and the liner would be cremated. However that is by the way. The funny side of the cardboard demonstration was, that I noticed from our exhibition stand this gent who was selling cardboard coffins had one model on two trestles. He was jumping up and down to show the people around him how strong it was. He was actually inside the coffin. I couldn't resist this any more and had to approach him on the subject. He asked me if I had a question to put to him. Being a Funeral Director I said."Nothing in particular but your customers must be more active than mine." "How does that come about?" he asked, I enquired if his customers were mostly English and he said they were. I then told him, "My customers are mostly Scottish and they don't jump up and down in their coffins. They just rest in peace."

A guid new year

He wanted a guid new year. In a wee Scottish village one of the local business men liked a good dram, in other words a wee drap o' the crater.

He always insisted when he passed on he would like everybody to have a drink on him. His instructions were that when we passed the local hotel which his good friend owned that the funeral procession would stop outside the hotel where the proprietor would have tables with any drink the mourners wanted. On the return journey the same would apply. They would also be given plenty of food. He said to his great friend, "And for you I want you to promise that every year on the night of Hogmanay you will pour a bottle of whisky over my grave for my New Year." He replied, "I certainly will providing you have no objection to it passing through my kidneys first.."

Ron Forbes, Illustrator's Christmas card to his undertaking friend.

The treasure hunt

The treasure hunt 1949.

This country family never had an illness in the family until the father took ill. To begin with he wasn't too bad, but he gradually got worse until he was confined to bed and had deteriorated in his mind quite a bit. His family were very worried about his condition especially the three sons. One day the eldest son said to his brothers, "We must act before he doesn't know anything. You remember all the metal biscuit boxes he had full of money. Where will they be?" The second son said, " I remember one was full of notes, some of them worth £50, £20 etc." The third son replied, "I remember when he was counting the money in the McVitie and Price box he let me touch it, It was full to the top with gold sovereigns and half sovereigns but where did he put them? Imagine if he dies and they are never found." At this point the eldest said, "Lets go to his bedroom and ask him. " As they entered he didn't seem to recognise them. The son said, "Father, you remember all the money you had in the boxes, where did you put them?" All he got was a moan and a groan and with that one hand fell from below the blankets with two fingers pointing to the floor. Having done this several times the sons decided they would put him in another room and dig up the floor. There they were with great mounds of soil from the excavation, stones etc., but alas no treasure. To their surprise later the father made a complete recovery from his illness. The eldest son approached him and asked him, "Father do you re- member when I asked you about the boxes of money and where they were hidden? You pointed two finger to the floor. On these instructions we dug the floor up only to find there was nothing there. Why did you confuse us?" "Na, na, lad," said the father "I didn't confuse you, I just didn't have the strength to point my two fingers up the way." Where is the Treasure?

1914 - 1918 First World War pals.

Two young lads were called to the forces and served together for the whole period of the war. Being demobbed together they bade each other a fond farewell, one went to Australia the other stayed in Britain. Forty five years passed when the one who had emigrated, after saving his money to come back to see his old comrade and great friend duly found his address and went to pay him a visit. When he knocked on the door a lady answered asking if she could help him. He said, "I've come to see my old pal Jimmy." She replied, "Oh what a shame you are just six weeks too late, he's passed on." Being very disappointed he said how sorry he was and commented how big a shock it must have been to her. "But what happened," he enquired. She said, "I asked him to go to the garden and cut a cabbage but he never came back. I went to find him. He was there dead as a door nail, "My goodness" he said "What a shock! What on earth did you do?" She said, "It was terrible! I just could hardly get over it, I just had to go to the expense of opening a big tin of peas." Just a tin of peas between him and the cabbage.

Thereby hangs the tails

Hereby hangs the tails. Having spoken earlier about how reverend tails look at a funeral, likewise a marriage. On this occasion my youngest daughter was being married in the village church. Her name being Elizabeth Taylor, her future husband Tommy Steele. This was mentioned in the papers on the morning of the wedding which makes you a wee bit apprehensive of what has to come. I had changed from the black waistcoat to the grey waistcoat, that being the difference between a wedding and a funeral with regards to the outfit, striped trousers and tails. I arrived at the church where quite a number of people were waiting to view. The photographer as usual got us into position, father and daughter posed for the birdie when somebody shouted from the crowd "Hello Undertaker, You might have taken your working clothes off for this occasion." At least I didn't have the black lum hat.

The expensive lie

The funeral director was called to a very large estate which
was situated at the top of a Scottish Glen. The deceased was
the Laird himself. The funeral director and his apprentice
had to travel approximately 40 miles to the mansion house.
They hadn't travelled very far when there were signs of
snow flakes beginning to fall. By the time they had arrived
at the destination it was a real white out. The snow was
forming into large drifts at either side of the road. This
meant that the funeral couldn't take place. The lairds
daughter then agreed to leave the funeral until the weather
had cleared and give the two men food and shelter.
But alas it was exactly eight days before the storm cleared
and the funeral could take place. During this time the
Funeral Undertaker and the Lady of the house became
friendly. The Funeral was completed and the undertaker
with his apprentice had just boarded the hearse.
The lady of the house approached and said to the Funeral
Director, "Would you be kind enough to give me your name
and address just in case I have to contact you." He said,
"That would be no problem," but having given careful
thought to this, he decided it could be a bit dangerous
and wrote down the apprentice's name and address. Nothing was heard until exactly nine months later when the
apprentice walked into the place of business and said to the

funeral director, "Do you remember when we did that funeral up the Glen and we stayed in the mansion house," He replied, "I don't want to hear about that at all - that's in the past. Anything you hear about that lady forget it. The apprentice said, "It's just that I can't understand how she got my name and address." The funeral director added, "That has nothing to do with me. Any correspondence you receive you will have to sort out yourself." The young lad replied, "I was thinking that it was such a shame, She was such a nice woman."

" Oh!" said the boss, "What has happened?" The apprentice replied, " She has just died and left me £92,000 and her estate. "

The Roadside story

In bygone days we had the local roadman or men who trimmed the grass verges on the country roads keeping the country side neat and tidy. In those days many a passer by would stop to have a chat just passing the time of day or to hear the news. This gentleman was having such a chat when in the distance he saw a funeral approaching.

He immediately fell to his knees at the same time removing his cap and bowing his head. The road man was taken aback with this procedure and said to him, " I've been a road man in the area for thirty five years and have seen many people pay their last respects but what you did was really the greatest. But why such a nice gesture?"

The gentleman replied, "Well it's the least I could do She was a grand wife to me."

Top deck view

Two ladies out for a bus trip having a good old chin wag
were placed on the top deck.

When they were passing the crematorium one lady said,
"You know my husband is in there." Her friend asked," oh!
does he work there?" She said, "He was cremated but
actually it was quite a story. He wanted to be buried but I
cremated him." Her friend replied, "You didn't carry out
his wish," "No," she said, " and I'll tell you something else.
To this day I don't think he is any the wiser."

At the ready

It was in June month. The weather was good. A lovely Summers day, when this funeral procession was travelling through the town. The hearse carrying the coffin was passing and there were two gentleman on the path way having a chin wag. One of them noticed on the top of the coffin was placed four bowls. One said, "I doubt he is to have his bowls buried with him." "No," said the other. "That's his wife being buried but he has a match immediately after the funeral."

The onlooker sees most of the game

The local funeral director was a keen viewer of sport on
television and on this occasion a football match Scotland v
England was due to start. He was looking forward to the
occasion and listening for the build up before kick off time.
In the funeral business anything can happen at any time
and it did. The need for help knock came to the door. There
stood four people requiring his services. Their loved one
had passed away. On entering the television was put into
darkness. He then proceeded to say he would get the necessary papers to finalise the arrangements At this point the
eldest of the family was looking at his watch was quite
agitated. and asked if he could possibly make the
arrangements at their house. It would be easier there as the
papers required were at hand. The bereaved by this time
were on their feet ready for the off. The funeral
director said he would be with them in approximately
twenty minutes. After having dressed according to the
situation he arrived at the deceased's house. Walking into
the room there they were to his surprise sitting around the
television. What were they watching? You would never
guess, - Scotland v England. He announced himself, passed
on his condolences and found himself a chair. He started to
take notes with great difficulty. At this point one of the

mourners said, "I hope the noise does not disturb you."
In between near misses he made little headway but worse
had to come, Scotland had scored, to a great eruption. How
the goal was scored had to be discussed thoroughly. The
funeral director, checking his notes, discovered in the
disturbance he had put down the venue for the funeral as
Hampden Park . Knowing it would be a big funeral and he
being in the theme of football must have felt like asking if
they wanted it all ticket. At this point he went to the next
room where the deceased was lying. Shutting the door he
looked at him and thought, "Your the only one that's with
it, at least you've reached your goal." Returning to the main
mourners stillness prevailed, England had scored. There
was a great hush in the room. With his pen at the ready he
was able to finalise the arrangements. The mourners stated
the reason for the arrangements at their house was to video
the match. As he left for home one of the next of kin came
to the door to bid him farewell. Forgetting himself the
mourner said, "Well when do we kick off on Wednesday?"
I think the funeral director should have played it at home
as there was no hope of a return. Final result 2.30p.m. on
Wednesday.

The Uprising

A couple who were pretty well on in years died within one day of each other. Their last wish was to lie in the chapel with their coffins open. During the service Mr and Mrs Hill were lying there, the minister had given his service and gave the organist the nod to play their favourite piece of music which was 'Ave Maria.' The church echoed to the beautiful tone of the organ when to the congregations astonishment Mr and Mrs Hill sat up in their coffins. The minister immediately stood up in the pulpit and announced, "Don't panic, there is nothing to worry about It's just THE HILLS ARE ALIVE WITH MUSIC."

A shirt on the wrong back

Two ministers were travelling by train from
Fraserburgh to a funeral in Aberdeen of one of the clergy.
In the same compartment on the seat opposite there was a
gentleman sitting very quietly reading his paper. The elder
of the two ministers had been forty years in his parish and
was telling the younger one how well he knew his parish
and everybody in it, parents, grandparents etc. The younger
of the two replied he had been eighteen months and was
beginning to know his parish and parishioners, much more
as time was going by. The older minister said, "You know it
takes a long time to know everything as I know it." The
gentleman who was sitting opposite minding his own
business but hearing all that was said looked over the top
of his paper and said "Aye minister, forty years, and you
know everybody and everything in your parish but I ken
something you dinna ken." "Oh!" said the minister, "And
what's that my man?"
"It's just my wife is your washer wife and I'm wearing your
shirt."

The No. 8 Jersey

A gentleman died in Glasgow, a prominent member of a Middle East family. His brother from Palestine flew over to make the funeral arrangements. By the time he arrived in Glasgow the Funeral Director had the situation well under control. He met the brother at the airport and took him to the funeral parlour. After discussing the various requirements he asked to see the deceased who was lying in his coffin. The Funeral Director removed the lid to allow the brother to view. There to his AMAZEMENT lay his dear departed in a complete Glasgow Rangers Football Strip. After this great surprise he asked, "Why is he dressed like that". The undertaker replied, "You see, being from the Middle East his last request was that he wanted to be buried in the GAZZA STRIP (Ghazir Strip).

Storm in the pew

A funeral service was being held in the local church. The type of weather that day was rather blustery, with quite a strong wind blowing towards the door. The next of kin were standing at the open door having a chat with the mourners as they came into the church. Sitting there four pews from the door was this rather nice old lady. The undertaker noticed she kept looking at the open door. Approaching her he said, "Excuse me madam but is the wind bothering you?" Aye she replied, "It is terrible but I'll be all right when the organ has started."

A surprising flush

A surprising flush

An elderly lady from the far north of Scotland who had stayed all her days on this very small croft and had none of the services such as electric light, tap water etc. She lost a dear friend who stayed in a small town in the south. After two days travelling she arrived for the funeral. Putting a switch down to light the light was something, to turn the tap on and out popped water was another. After attending the funeral she was invited back to the house for tea. Before sitting down at the table she asked where the Watery was. (The Scottish word for toilet). Being a tenement block the toilet was situated at the rear of the building through a mutual corridor. All the people in that landing used the same facilities. Approximately one hour after leaving the rest of the mourners someone had noticed she had never returned so went to investigate. To their surprise she was sitting on the toilet shaking like a leaf. When asked what was wrong she said, looking up at the pull chain, "I don't know what my trouble is, but every time I pull myself up with that chain the water just pours from me."

Ancient mode of transport being used in modern times by T. Cribb & Sons. Funeral Directors & Carriage Masters, Canning Town, London.

A quick exit

A Church dedicated as St. Conon's Chapel and Burial
Ground - Later known as ST. Murdochs.

The story is told of a gentleman who wanted to buy a piece
of ground for burial in this small cemetery or kirkyard
situated on the Angus coast line between Ethie Haven and
Auchmithie. These are fascinating little fishing villages,
like the rest of that coast line it teems with history and
fantastic tales of the past. This gentleman having a pin leg
was known to most as 'the pinner' and had a strong belief
that one day every corpse would rise from their graves and
walk. During his purchase of ground he demanded to be
interred at the gate. The seller of the ground looked at his
plan of the cemetery and said "your ground will be next to
the gate but why did you request that plot? " He replied,
"When the last trumpet- sounds on the day of judgement
everybody will rise from their graves. Can you imagine the
mad rush for the gate when they all rise and me with a pin
leg that bit slower." At least this way I will have a leg start
on them." It was then known as the Pinners Gate.

The Umbrella

The Umbrella that went down instead of up.

On a very cold, blustery day in mid winter with lots
of snow a service was being held in the village cemetery.
This service was slightly different from usual.
The mourners were walking around the grave on the
wooden planks provided for the cord holders to stand on
when they lower the coffin. In this case the coffin was
sitting on the wooden palls that the bearers had used for
carrying the coffin to the grave. Overhanging the grave was
quite a large branch of an adjoining tree. The service
proceeded but as they walked around the grave an elderly
gentleman who was carrying an umbrella slipped. As he
tried to save himself he dropped his umbrella passed the
side of the coffin and into the grave. This was rather an
embarrassing situation for the party concerned. I, as the
undertaker, thought, "Let's carry on as if nothing had
happened." Alas! the driver of the hearse arrived at the
grave with a rope which was kept with the vehicle in case
of emergency. The elderly gentleman noticed the rope and
to add to the situation he had formed a big noose on the
end of same. I'm sure the mourner wondered as he looked
up at the over hanging branch above him if this was the
punishment for dropping an umbrella in a grave.
To everybody's surprise and while the service was still in

progress, the man with the rope lay down on his stomach and proceeded to drop the noose over the handle of the umbrella with great success. After the service we went to a hotel for a cuppa and refreshment. Jokingly I remarked to the gentleman that I thought he was trying to cut out the middle man, a sort of do it yourself and asking if he hurt himself. Putting his hand to his deaf ear he said, "Oh aye, but nothing a large whisky widna cure". Humour is expensive even in old age.

Bats in the Belfry

Three ministers were having a cup of tea after a friend's funeral. They were discussing various items of importance concerning their Churches. During their conversation they discovered they all had Bats in their Belfrys and were having a problem getting rid of them.

The first Minister said that he had borrowed a double barrel shotgun and fired it to frighten the Bats. It cost him quite a bit of money to repair the damage he had caused to the roof only to find the Bats were still in the Belfry.

The second Minister commented that he had released a canister of a horrible smelling substance thinking this would clear them out. He found in the morning that they were still there as **bold** as ever.

The third Minister said that he had no problem ridding his Belfy of Bats. "How on earth did you manage that?" asked his friends. He replied, "It was very simple. I went up to the Belfry at midnight and gave them my Blessing. The next evening I went back and made them all members of my Church. You know, I haven't seen a Bat since."

Business is slack

The village undertaker was taking a walk when he met one of the local residents who asked him if he was busy. The reply came back, "No, the very opposite. I haven't buried a living soul for a fortnight."

The Flying Undertaker

The flying Undertaker

Another story told to me by one of my undertaking friends. It concerned his grandfather who was a well liked gentleman, one of the old breed who had been carrying out funerals for many years. Being quite near to the Angus Glens a lot of difficult journeys had to be made in those early days. Everything was horse drawn and when going to the top of the glens they had an arrangement with the farmers en- route, that being quite a journey they would change horses at various distances both going and coming back from the funeral. As time passed by and things began to change to motorised transport the grandfather decided it was time to make a move. At that time there were no motorised hearses to be bought, so he did the next best thing. He purchased one of the early motor cars and proceeded to cut the body to take the glass case off the horse drawn hearse. This he had done with great difficulty and had made progress. Everything was now in place except the mudguards, as they were called in these days, the wings as they are known today. As he was working away an elderly gentleman looked into the joiner's work-shop. In these days there were very few people who were undertakers only. They were usually cabinetmakers, joiners and undertakers. The reason being there were no manufacturers as such and the coffins had to be made.

That was done by the trades who were qualified to carry out such tasks. He was feeling quite proud of his workmanship and asked the onlooker what he thought of his work. The man replied, "Its a' right but what are you doing." He explained about the transfer of the glass case and all he had to do was fix on the wings and that was the machine complete. The gentleman went home to his croft in the Glen, explained to his wife about the visit, repeating several times that the undertaker was a wonderful forethinking man. She replied, "What is so special about him." He told her about the conversion, and added, "He must be to take them all the road now, he's putting wings on his hearse."

Cash Deposited

A wealthy gentleman died and his wife wanted to make sure his last journey would go smoothly for his crossing over. She approached the undertaker saying she would like a large sum of cash to be put in the coffin to pay all expenses on his last journey. Having several banking accounts, she telephoned each bank to have the cash delivered to the house so that it could be placed in the coffin beside him. One security van arrived, then another. The cash was unloaded and the undertaker started to place the money in the coffin beside him only to discover he couldn't get it all in. He asked the lady if she would mind if he counted the money in her presence. Having checked same, the total amount came to thousands of pounds. He suggested that he would remove the money and replace it with a cheque. Having done this, he told his book-keeper who panicked and replied, "I hope it doesn't go through the bank before you get that cash deposited".

Farewell to a young Black Watch Soldier

The Creamtorium Srevice was conducted by the Padre with the Colonel and R.S.M. in attendance. The Padre was led by a lone piper who played 'The Flowers o' the Forest'. His family was so proud that his Regiment had given him such a fitting farewell, all dressed immaculate in their Highland Uniforms.

The Lum Hat

It is old fashioned but we still carry out the old tradition such as carrying the coffin where possible, striped trousers, waistcoat and tails. And to top everything a tile or in Scotland a Lum Hat hence the heading the title of a Scottish song.

As I said earlier that dress has still got proper respect but alas accidents happen. Having worn my hat quite a long time unknown to me the threads on the inside rim that is joined to the hat had worn with the sweat through the years. Having walked in front of the hearse I was standing very reverend until the hearse passed me and came to rest at that point. I removed my tile hat only to discover I had only removed part of it. I was unaware that the two inch band was left sticking to my head, the main part in my hand. As one of the mourners passed me he said "Your the only funeral director I've ever seen with a halo." Looking in the glass of the hearse I realised what had happened. It didn't suit me at all!

The Elephant Rock

Officially they are called Boddin Point and Rock of St Skae, but locally folk will understand better if you say "The Bodin" and "The Elephant Rock." You can get there by road, but a more exciting route follows the clifftop from Buckie Den at the north end of Lunan Bay.

The Rickle Craig with its rocky pinnacles makes a dramatic bit of coastal scenery, and is much loved by seabirds - especially shags, fulmars, petrels and herring gulls.

Farther on, the cliffs dwindle away, and The Bodin is a level promontory, long famous for its salmon fishing station and its old sea-battered lime kilns. A fine place for a picnic, incidentally.

The Elephant Rock lies within easy walking distance farther along the coast-but "lies" is hardly the right word, for it's an upstanding headland abutting on the foreshore. Nothing unusual about that, but the form of it is amusingly remarkable, it's so obviously like an elephant!

Trunk, Head, limbs, sides and back - all are there. And strange, or even crazy, though it seems, a tiny burial place is set on the elephant's rump right above the tail.

One day when I was there, with the tide farther in than in my drawing, it looked just like an elephant having a drink at a water hole.

A remarkable piece of sculpture from Nature's studio.

The elephant's graveyard is easily reached from its tail end. There are traces of a chapel, as well as the graves of departed Arkleys of nearby Dunninald, Keiths of Usan, and Scotts of Abbeythrone.

On my first visit to this tiny graveyard by the sea, it was pointed out to me that, according to the inscription on one

of the stones, the occupant of the grave had died before he was born.

The dates are now difficult to read. A pity, for it added a unique touch to the interesting but tenuous link between the burial place and St Skae.

Who St Skae was, nobody seems to know, but the name Skae is mindful of the word

In Memory of
George James Ramsay
Born Nov 24th 1850
Died Dec 17th 1840

skeir, meaning simply rock or cliff, and that may hold a clue.

Like St Kilda in the Outer Herbrides, it's possible that St Skae never existed!

Finally

To finalise what I hope will give a little insight to the lighter side of being a Funeral Undertaker and at the same time knowing that it is only through bereavement these stories have come about.

There are many people I would like to thank over almost fifty years especially the many families who entrusted me to carry out the last rites of their loved ones. I consider this a privilege and honour to be entrusted with such a duty.

I must show my gratitude to the many other people who carry out their services when I have required some assistance and have always been at hand to help. To thank them individually would require another book as they stretch from the South of England to the North of Scotland. Amongst them are the clergy for adding their comforting touch when most needed also the people who prepare the last resting place in Cemetery (Kirkyard) or Crematorium. They have always given great attention to their duties, being properly carried out.

The Doctors and Nurses of the medical profession have given their full attention at all times. What would a service in Church or whatever be without music? The person who is so often taken for granted is the organist. To the Police Force in general for their willingness to help.

If I've missed you out please forgive me but you can be assured you are in my thanks somewhere.

Last but not least. What is a good business without a good back up? I mean a good and trusted lady behind the scenes. I make reference to my wife.

Thank you for reading my book, and I hope to see you SOON.

The caring approach to a sensitive subject